IN A HIGH
SPIRITUAL
SEASON

IN A HIGH
SPIRITUAL
SEASON

JOAN CHITTISTER

Triumph™ Books
Liguori, Missouri

Published by Triumph™ Books
Liguori, Missouri
An Imprint of Liguori Publications

Excerpts reprinted from *The Monastic Way*, with permission of Mount Saint Benedict Monastery, 6101 East Lake Road, Erie, PA 16511. (Individual subscriptions are available.)

Library of Congress Cataloging-in-Publication Data

Chittister, Joan
    In a high spiritual season / Joan Chittister—1st ed.
        p. cm.
    ISBN: 0-89243-775-8
    1. Meditations. 2. Benedictine nuns—Religious life.
3. Religious life—Catholic authors.   I. Title.
BX2182.2.C525 1995
242—dc20

94-40339
CIP

Copyright © 1995 by Joan Chittister
Printed in the United States of America
First Edition 1995
96 96 97 98 99   5 4 3 2 1

This book is dedicated to

Audrey Hirt

whose relentless search
for women's wisdom
is a model to us all.

*I*T is so easy to forget that new seasons in life take preparation and, sometimes, long, slow periods of waiting and long, calm bursts of patience in a world that wants instant answers and on-the-spot remedies. We all like to engineer life. It is time to learn simply to live it at its own pace.

IN SUMMER
Warmth Radiates

L IFE is physically easier now and spiritually pregnant with possibility. Warmth becomes a way of life that makes us open to new people and new experiences; flowers confront us with our responsibility for beauty. Finding God in nature is a very monastic thing.

$\mathcal{T}$HINGS change in the summertime, even in a monastery. In June, in particular, you can see how the seasons affect our lives. The community takes time away from the regular rounds of ministry to make its annual retreat together; the inner courtyard blooms quietly but riotously; the Sisters spend more time walking in the woods and sitting together beside the lake at night watching sunsets. Some of us fish; some of us plant; some of us read in the sun. People we haven't seen for the whole long winter reappear again; the children return to camp; the families begin to visit; the chapel and dining room are full of old friends and new visitors just passing through.

Clearly, June is the time for being in the world in new ways, for throwing off the cold and dark spots of life.

❧

$\mathcal{I}$MAGINE how happy, how holy, life would be if we ever really learn to see beauty.

*A*LFRED Lord Tennyson, the English poet, wrote, "'Tis better to have loved and lost, than never to have loved at all." Sometimes it's true: we lose something we have loved. And who knows why? What is really important in the end is that, having lost a love, we never lose either the measure of its quality or the depth of its learnings. This is the immortal dimension of every friendship, its bridge between us and the rest of the world, the everlasting mark of friendship on what we call ourselves, the tinder of what it has inspired in us forever.

❧

*I*T is so easy to want the good in life, but not so easy to make the changes it will take to achieve it. We want to lose weight, but we don't eat less. We want to get a promotion, but we don't want to work longer hours. We want to live a more balanced life, but we don't want to stop anything we're doing now.

The fact is that we really want other things more. The question, then, is not *Why can't I find time to exercise?* The question is *What do I really want far more than I want to lose weight?*

*J*EALOUSY is the other person's problem. My problem is to build an inner life so rich that it cannot be destroyed when those who want what I have finally get it.

❧

*T*HE sign of complete serenity in life is to be able to lose all the externals and not notice. Seventeenth-century theologian and poet Angelus Silesius wrote, "One has not lived in vain who learns to be unruffled by loss, by gain, by joy, by pain."

❧

*T*HERE is nothing we can lose in life that does not teach us something worth knowing. Sometimes we learn to pick our friends more carefully. Sometimes we learn not to be so committed to what the world calls "success." Sometimes we learn that we have been about the wrong things entirely in life. But there is no such thing as failure as long as we learn something from it. Or, as French essayist Michel de Montaigne wrote, "There are some defeats more triumphant than victories."

*W*E must never sacrifice principle to short-term approval. It is a life lesson hard-won on the institutional ladders, cocktail parties, and coffee klatsches of the world, but it may be the only lesson worth learning at all.

❧

*I*T is so easy to hate what exposes us for what we are. We are not the vocalist we would like to be so we hate the person who can really sing. We are not the star we wanted to be so we hate the stars around us and work against them and try to bring them down. Jealousy corrodes the soul.

Look carefully at what you hate without cause. It may be telling you a great deal about yourself.

❧

*T*HE rights and opportunities of women have always been limited by institutions and nations that called themselves just. If monasteries of women demonstrate anything social at all, it may well be the essential competence, independence, and spiritual beauty of women. Why do you suppose that the world so routinely overlooks that?

"*A* fox dressed up in sheep's clothing," the rabbis say, "is still a fox." There are some people, some situations, that are simply not worth wrenching our own lives to convert. The die is cast. Their minds are made up. They don't want to change; they can't change, and they won't change here, now, for you. But that's all right. Give your energies where they'll do the most good.

Are you wasting your life on something like that right now?

❧

A Malayan proverb teaches: "Don't assume that simply because the water is calm that there are no crocodiles in it." It's when we put our trust in a situation itself for our sense of well-being and achievement that we jeopardize both our happiness and our future.

Do well whatever you need to do at the time, but do not give your entire life to that which is not permanent.

*A*N Arab proverb teaches: "I must set my face to the wind and scatter my handful of seeds. It is no big thing to scatter seeds, but I must have the courage to keep on facing the wind."

Where in life are you facing the most opposition? Don't flinch. Who knows when the wind will change?

❧

*T*HE important thing in life is to have a center so sound that nothing outside ourselves can disturb it.

❧

"*I* have kept my little rule and maintained my little fasts and said my little prayers faithfully," the disciple said to the holy one. "Now what can I do to be enlightened?" And the holy one stood up and stretched her arms to heaven. "Why not," she said, spreading her fingers wide, "why not be completely turned into fire?"

"THE heart has its reasons which reason does not understand," wrote French philosopher Blaise Pascal. Beauty defies logic; heartwarming compassion defies logic; logic defies logic.

The fact is that it is feeling, not logic, that fires life with energy and fills life with meaning.

TRY saying this silently to everyone and everything you see for thirty days and see what happens to your own soul: *I wish you happiness now and whatever will bring happiness to you in the future.* If we said it to the sky, we would have to stop polluting. If we said it when we see the ponds and lakes and streams, we would have to stop using them as garbage dumps and sewers. If we said it to small children, we would have to stop abusing them, even in the name of training. If we said it to people, we would have to stop stoking the fires of enmity around us. Beauty and human warmth would take root in us like a clear, hot June day. We would change.

*A*N Aztec song goes: *I offer flowers. I sow flower seeds. I plant flowers. I assemble flowers. I pick flowers. I pick different flowers. I seek flowers. I offer flowers....I clothe him in flowers. I cover her in flowers. I love them with flowers.*

Have you loved anyone with flowers yet this month? Why not today—before it's too late?

❧

*D*ON'T take anything for granted. All of us must recommit ourselves to the goals of our lives every single day, or the fire of life may well go out in us.

❧

*H*ELEN Keller, the woman who triumphed over the childhood loss of sight, hearing, and speech to become an author and lecturer, said, "The world is full of suffering. It is also full of the overcoming of it." And because of the way she herself dealt with those losses, millions of similarly challenged people after her have lived fuller lives. And she did it all with only smell and touch, with flowers and warmth.

*A*MERICAN poet and abolitionist Lucy Larcom wrote, "If the world seems cold to you, kindle fires to warm it." Is there a cold spot in your life right now—struggles with a family member, sadness, the pain of a disappointment? What fire can you kindle today to ease its impact on the rest of life?

*T*HE prayer from Mary Lou Kownacki's *The Sacred in the Simple* calls the community to new energy at the breakpoint of every day. It reads: "Let not the heat of the noonday sun wither my spirit or lay waste my hopes. May I be ever green, a strong shoot of justice, a steadfast tree of peace."

*I*N the Philippines, a political prisoner wrote on the wall of his cell, "Those who would give light must endure burning." No one gets away easy. If you are about something worthwhile, it will be tested by fatigue and pressure and the sheer boredom of the daily.

When did you want to give up but persevered? Was it the thing you should have done? How do you know?

*L*IFE's major problem does not lie in choosing good from evil. That's obvious and easy. No, life's real problem comes in choosing good from good. What's the answer? That's also easy: when values are in conflict, always choose the higher one.

❧

*P*OPULAR comedian and actress Lily Tomlin said, "Once poor, always wantin' rich is just a way of wantin' *bigger*." When we know our poverties, we can ask for help. Other-wise, we are inclined to think that we can be self-sufficient. Then, we take care of ourselves first.

❧

*T*HE need for security can be such a block in life. It keeps us where we are, yes; but, worse, it can keep us from discovering where we must be if we are ever to grow to full stature.

What is security doing for you at this time in your life?

*I*T's possible to have too much in life. Too many clothes jade our appreciation for new ones; too much money can put us out of touch with life; too much free time can dull the edge of the soul. We need sometimes to come very near the bone so that we can taste the marrow of life rather than its superfluities.

*P*EOPLE want change, but they want it to come without discomfort. They want to rock no boats, make no waves. They think that people can be talked into change. The fact is that most people only change when they have no choice.

Think of the great attitudinal changes in your life. What incidents happened that made change necessary? What kind of things are you yourself doing to bring necessary changes now? After all, one of the functions of leadership is to lead.

*T*RUST is the counterpoint of generosity. I can only give my own possessions to someone who needs them more than I do if I truly believe that by God's goodness, they will come back to me when I need them too. Generosity is easy. It makes us look good. It's trust that's hard to come by.

Somewhere there is a squirrel in each of us, hoarding, preserving, hiding, against the unseen winters of life. Then it's time, perhaps, to remember nineteenth-century American poet Celia Laighton Thaxter's dictum: "Sad soul, take comfort, nor forget that sunrise never failed us yet."

❧

*T*ODAY, give away something you value. It will enrich the life of another and it will liberate you as well.

❧

*V*ISION, sacrifice, and hope are the caretakers of the future. Without them, tomorrow is impossible and today is straw. We don't do things because we know we'll succeed. We do them because they must be done.

*K*ATERI Tekakwitha was martyred in 1680. While white Westerners were debating whether or not Indians and Blacks were fully human, Kateri was defying every definition we erroneously held "savage." She was perpetually devout; she took a private vow of virginity and exercised complete control over her passions—something we said was impossible for nonwhites to do and therefore refused to admit them to convents and seminaries. To the French, Kateri became a clear, immovable witness to the spiritual integrity of native people and a sign to them of the greatness of the One God. She prevailed against every odd simply by refusing to quit. Kateri is a great example for the long haul.

❧

A Zen saying goes: "O snail climb Mount Fuji but slowly, slowly." If we are to persevere for the long haul, we must not overdrive our souls. We must immerse ourselves in good music, good reading, great beauty, and peace, so that everything good in us can rise again and lead us on beyond disappointment, beyond boredom, beyond criticism, beyond loss.

*T*HE long haul we're facing in this generation is a change of national priorities, a redefinition of human values. That will take speaking out over and over again, even when no one wants to hear about it anymore. But everyone of us needs a moon to aim for. Do what it takes to give yourself the energy to keep on speaking out.

∞

*W*HEN the soul is heavy and the work seems futile, a visit to an art museum—where art and beauty run rampant, and meetings, proposals, finances, and debate have no place—revives the heart and makes it soft. Then going on seems possible. Then life has vision again. Then going on seems necessary.

∞

A spirituality without a prayer life is no spirituality at all, and it will not last beyond the first defeat. Prayer is an opening of the self so that the Word of God can break in and make us new. Prayer unmasks. Prayer converts. Prayer impels. Prayer sustains us on the way. Pray for the grace it will take to continue what you would like to quit.

*T*HE first woman to pilot an airplane alone across the Atlantic Ocean, Amelia Earhart, was born in 1897. What people said a woman couldn't do and shouldn't do, she did. She showed the world the kind of courage that does not blink in the face of impossibility and does not waver despite the odds.

*P*ROPHETS are so dangerous because they cry in season and out of season, politely and impolitely, loud and long.

"*I* give you my naked soul like a statue unveiled," wrote Uruguayan poet Juana De Ibarboubou. Would anyone know your naked soul if they saw it? Do you know it yourself?

*T*HERE is a very thin line between taking care of myself and being selfish. To discover the difference, ask yourself why you are doing what you are doing. And tell yourself the truth.

*N*OVELIST Diane Johnson writes, "We are surrounded by the enraged." These words have a prophetic ring to them. Every day the number of inhumanely poor increases. Only love equally enraged can possibly restore the balance. What will you give of yourself to begin to reestablish it?

❧

*M*ONASTIC mindfulness has as much to do with being aware of where God is *not* being allowed to work in the world as it does with being aware of where God clearly is. We must be aware, for instance, that the people of poor countries are starving, that rich countries have the food, and that poor countries can't pay for it. We have to be aware that God did not create the world for half of us to starve the other half.

What values would have to change in the United States for God to be able to work in this situation?

❧

*W*E must become aware of God where we are and in what we do, or life will never really be sacred to us.

*A*WARENESS of the sacred in life is what holds our world together, and the lack of aware-ness of the sacred is what is tearing it apart.

❧

*T*HE Feast of the Assumption, the moment of Mary's final and total absorption into God, makes us aware of our own irrevocable end. And to keep the end in mind is a very monastic thing. It is the end, after all, that makes every present moment meaningful.

❧

*T*WO ideas militate against our consciously contributing to a better world. The idea that we can do everything or the conclusion that we can do nothing to make this globe a better place to live are both temptations of the most insidious form. One leads to arrogance; the other to despair. We can, however, be mindful of our own worlds and so, perhaps, make others more mindful of theirs.

*C*ANDLES and vigil lights remind us al ways of the ebb of our lives. They tell us that day is slipping by. They tell us that it is time to look into the dark spots of our souls and bring light there. They teach us not to burn the candle at both ends. They remind us that we have no light to give to others unless we first of all have it in ourselves.

❧

*C*ONTEMPLATION is the ability to see the world around us as God sees it. Contemplation is a sacred mindfulness of my holy obligation to care for the world I live in. Contemplation is awareness of God within me and in the people around me. Contemplation is consciousness of the real fullness of life. God is calling me on and on and on, beyond all these partial things, to the goodness of the whole of life and my responsibility to it.

❧

*S*EPTEMBER has a strange and wonder ful feeling. It is the best part of the summer and the hardest part of the summer. Just when summer gets perfect—fresh nights, soft sun, casual breezes, crushingly full and quietly cooling trees, empty beaches, and free weekends—it ends.

Life is like that too. Just when we get it right, it starts to change. The job gets easy and we know just how to do it, and they tell us we're retired. The children grow up and get reasonable and they leave home, just when it's nice to have them around. The days get less full of work, but we're older now and too stiff to play. The money we never had enough of to spend on clothes abounds after the mortgage is paid off, but the body has lost the shape for the style. That's diminishment. That's life on the edge of autumn. And that's beautiful—if we have the humility for it.

❧

*H*UMILITY is a natural virtue. It's one of those things that everybody has to get eventually or else die in misery. Diminishment, for instance, is one of the facts of life that breeds humility. Diminishment is part of every experience. We get to practice it all our lives. And sometimes we understand it and sometimes we don't.

*A*CCORDING to the Rule of Saint Benedict, the third rung on the ladder of humility is the ability to submit ourselves to the wisdom of another. There is nothing that diminishes the ego so well as to admit that someone else's way is at least as good as our own.

❧

*G*RANDMA Moses, born in 1860, is remembered for her paintings. But Grandma Moses never even began to paint until she was in her late seventies. Now, tell us again how you're too old to start to do something new, something exciting, something of value. Let's hear no more of the diminishment we impose on ourselves.

❧

*M*ARY, the Mother of Jesus, was in awe of God and saw God's will as better for her than the conventions of the society in which she lived. She accepted the invitation to be the Mother of God. Because of that kind of humility—of self-knowledge—we were all given the chance to rise above our otherwise diminished selves to become Christ bearers in our own time.

$\mathcal{J}$F anything diminishes a person, it is the cancer of constant complaining. What did you complain about today? Did that make it any better? Did it make you a more pleasant person to be around?

❧

$\mathcal{H}$UMILITY tells us not to arrogantly replace custom or wisdom figures or history or experience. It tells us to learn from those who have gone before us. Psychiatrist Karen Horney wrote, "Life itself still remains a very effective therapist."

❧

$\mathcal{N}$OT being the first to speak, not being the last to pronounce on a subject, takes a lot of discipline; but it gains a lot of information that may someday turn into wisdom.

❧

$\mathcal{H}$ILDEGARD of Bingen, a Benedictine abbess of the thirteenth century, was a scholar, a counselor, a mystic, and a preacher. She was deeply involved with the social issues of her culture and all the major figures of her time; popes and kings alike corresponded with her, seeking her ideas and advice. She published the only medical encyclopedias of her day, and her theological insights have become as popular in this decade as in her own.

Hildegard was a woman of her time and a woman for her time. She poured herself out all her life. She was a truly humble woman who knew her gifts and developed them to the benefit of all of us. No false diminishment here. Maybe she ought to be the patron saint of the women's movement.

❧

*T*HE degrees of humility, presented in the sixth-century Rule of Saint Benedict, are a ladder of relationships. They teach us how to relate to God, to ourselves, and to others. They start us in the presence of God, tell us to learn from others in life, and instruct us to deal tenderly with others. They tell us to walk through life in the presence of God, accepting ourselves and respecting the similar weaknesses, gifts, and struggles of others. They are a blueprint for peace, for happiness, for getting drunk on the present in life.

P RECISELY because of the greatness of God, we don't have to be great at all. Just in awe.

In Autumn
Grace Abounds

*T*HE skill of life lies in harvesting well and harvesting always, in taking the best that life has to give at any state, in being patient with ourselves along the way.

*L*IFE is a thing of many stages and moving parts. What we do with ease at one time of life we can hardly manage at another. What we could not fathom doing when we were young, we find great joy in when we are old. Like the seasons through which we move, life itself is a never-ending series of harvests, a different fruit for every time.

The secret of life is to let every segment of it produce its own yield at its own pace. Every period has something new to teach us. The harvest of youth is achievement; the harvest of middle-age is perspective; the harvest of age is wisdom; the harvest of life is serenity.

❧

*S*AINT Thérèse of Lisieux, the French Carmelite nun who made the simple things of life the seedbed of her sanctity, was also one of the first women who declared her desire to be a priest. "Since I cannot be a priest on earth," she wrote, "I would prefer to go to heaven." God, who had no place for inequities in heaven, would in due time, she knew, bring to ripeness the spiritual gifts of women.

A proverb reads: "Nothing we do changes the past, but everything we do changes the future." The fact is that building the future, planting for the next generation to harvest, is what every generation is about. What are we leaving to the children of our time?

E LEANOR Roosevelt once said, "Life was meant to be lived....One must never turn a back on life." To fail to take a position on one of life's great questions is to turn our back on life. It is, as a matter of fact, a decision to turn our back on the next generation.

N OW is life's harvesttime, whatever your age. Enjoy it.

O N the East Coast, November is a sear month, beautiful for its bleakness. The skies hang gray and heavy, the wind gnaws and bellows. Life changes drastically from the velvet days of early autumn. The things we love begin to die right before our eyes. The roses begin to shrivel on the bush, the sun draws away, the colors around us start to darken. Then the streets get quieter, the neighbors disappear inside their houses, and the days darken before the light has had time to seep through the mist of morning. The earth rests.

Autumn is a time of great life learnings. We learn that we cannot control the passage of time in life. We learn to accept each of the stages of life with serenity. We learn to look to new moments in life with hope rather than despair.

※

*T*HE *Dhammapada*, a Hindu scripture, teaches: "There are those who forget that death will come to all. For those who remember, quarrels come to an end." Life is made up of millions upon millions of fragile moments wasted on struggles that in the end don't count at all.

What quarrel have you continued far too long? What would happen if you stopped it?

*W*E know who we are, we know what we've done in life, we know that the way we act every moment is the measure of our life. God will not expect more of us than we know we should expect of ourselves.

❧

*D*OROTHY Day, who founded the Catholic Worker Movement and lived and worked among the poor until she was eighty-three, wrote, "No one has a right to sit down and feel hopeless. There's too much work to do." If American society is guilty of anything, it is guilty of ignoring the wisdom and experience of age. As a result, too many people go into professional retirement feeling hopeless when they should be beginning to feel really confident and useful in life.

Don't let your enthusiasm and participation die young.

❧

*I*F death teaches us anything, it teaches us that everything will some day end. The lesson, of course, is to wear suffering well, hold beauty lightly, and fear nothing.

O F everything we must learn to accept in life, accepting ourselves may be the hardest of them all. Accepting the fact that we are average people in a world of giants, that we are adequate people in a world of geniuses, that we are wounded people in a world that touts perfection, is not easy. Accepting, too, however, that we have everything we need to live happy lives if we can simply stop wanting more, is even harder. Have you done that yet?

❧

L IFE is a series of small deaths. We lose jobs and get left by people and move out of cities and get overlooked for promotions and see our dreams dissolve in midair. Those things are as sure in life as death itself. The only question every small and separate death confronts us with is "Are we willing to believe that we will rise again?"

S TUBBLE in a cornfield, brown leaves on dry husks, brittle yellow stalks where once gold silk had been, are some of the saddest scenes November has to offer. They are also the breeding ground of hope.

What has gone to stubble in your own life that is also a sign of coming life?

❧

A CCEPTANCE is one of the richer exercises of life. It is not to be universally prescribed, and it is not to be confused with passivity. Some things are never to be accepted: violence is not to be accepted; injustice is never to be accepted; human destruction is never to be accepted.

But most of the hard things of life come out of circumstances, not out of malice. Then the ability to accept life as it is becomes the ability to make life better. Accept what is, and ask what you gained from acceptance. The answer, surely, will be serenity.

❧

O NE of the most poignant of our community customs is the Celebration of Memories ceremony. The night before a Sister is buried, the community gathers at her coffin to remember the moments of her life that taught us all something about life. The simple ritual turns death into life at the very moment we feel its loss most. It is a model, this finding life in loss, for dealing with death of all kinds.

ZEN teaches that once upon a time a disciple asked the holy woman, Sono, what needed to be done to put the human heart at rest. "Every morning and every evening, whenever anything at all happens to you," the woman said, "just keep on saying, 'Thank you for everything. I have no complaint whatsoever.'"

The man did as he was instructed for an entire year but then came back to Sono disappointed that nothing had really changed in his life. "What you told me to do failed," he said. "What should I do now?"

And Sono said immediately, "Thank you for everything. I have no complaint whatsoever."

On hearing these words, the man was able to open his spiritual eye and returned home with great joy.

The thing to remember now is that the celebration of Thanksgiving began when there was really very little to be thankful for.

*I*N a high spiritual season, we are more drawn to prayer. But we must learn to be very careful, for prayer can be an easy substitute for real spirituality. It would be impossible to have spirituality without prayer, of course, but it is certainly possible to pray without having a spirituality at all. How do you know? "Am I becoming kinder?" is a good place to start.

*T*HE stores are crowded with shoppers; the displays seduce us into buying and buying. And there is nothing wrong with giving, as God's grace is given to us in life. What is wrong is thinking that things given once a year are a substitute for presence and care the rest of the year.

Is there someone on your Christmas list whom you only remember with a yearly present?

*W*E often complain that our lives are too busy. And yet, every Sunday is supposed to be a day of rest. That means one-seventh of life is rest: 52 days a year which equals 3,640 days in seventy years—or ten years of Sabbath, rest, and reflection in a lifetime. Sabbath is that period of holy leisure when I take time to look at life in fresh, new ways. This Sunday, forget the Christmas "to do" list.

ॐ

"COME, O Wisdom from above," the Church prays in preparation for Christmas. Wisdom is the ability to see the world as God sees it. Try reading the newspaper today through the eyes of God who was born in a stable, counted to be of no account, hounded by society from one place to another.

ॐ

AMERICAN novelist Margaret Runbeck wrote, "Happiness is not a state to arrive at, but a manner of traveling." Everybody has a choice: we can enjoy all the waitings of our lives and take them as appreciation points, or we can fill them with agitation and resentment.

What are you waiting for in life at this time? Are you making it good time or bad?

*A*NGELS hover over life, tantalizing in their auras of mystical goodness, magnetic in their possibilities. Everybody wants to have an angel. The Christmas challenge, however, is to bring everybody to want to *be* an angel. While you are waiting for your angel to appear in life, plan to be a watchful presence for someone else.

*I*F what we wait for is not within us in the first place, we wait in vain. To wait with anxiety for peace is never to be peaceful. To wait for public success without feeling good about ourselves is to never know achievement. To wait for the spiritual life without a continuing sense of the presence of God is to be consumers of religion, perhaps, but to miss its meaning.

"COME, O Sacred One of Israel," the Advent liturgy prays. It's a shame that we limit the sacred to religious objects or special places. Here we are reminded that the Sacred One is becoming human and, in so doing, breathes sacredness into every human life. Make an inward bow to each person you meet today.

❧

"COME, O Key of David," we sing during the Advent season. This antiphon is a searing cry for the kind of Christian commitment that opens doors and breaks down barriers between peoples. It calls us to devote ourselves to bringing unity to a divided world. Try to unlock one door that is keeping someone locked out of your heart.

❧

THE Christmas season is a gift in itself. It releases us from the priorities of ordinary time and gives us the right to party more and pray more and love more. Be sure you give yourself this Christmas gift.

IN WINTER
Hearts Touch

*P*EOPLE need physical hospitality, spiritual hospitality, and psychological hospitality always. There must always be someone available to care for anyone and everyone in need. The winter cold reminds us to open our hearts always. Someone is waiting to get in.

*U*NLESS we come to reverence others in our lives, we will never really give ourselves in their behalf. Worse than that, we ourselves will miss the beauty of life.

❧

*W*HAT we do to other people can affect their own way of being in the world. In other words, the attention and dignity we give to those around us is the seed of all the relationships in the world.

❧

*W*E need to begin to see women everywhere differently. We need to begin to see all women as bearers of the grace of God and bringers of the Word. That would be a new beginning that could change the world again.

❧

*K*EEPING up enthusiasm and kindness at the end of a workweek is a gift of enormous proportions. It makes life new for everyone.

*W*E need to learn to give needy people our full attention, not simply our donations of old clothes and change.

❧

A person can get a lot of satisfaction out of keeping rules. It may be precisely when we get most wrapped up in the rules that we may have the most to learn about real spirituality. When Saint Scholastica prevailed on her brother, Saint Benedict, to spend more time in conversation with her rather than return on time to his monastery, it was because she knew that Benedict needed more reflection than he needed rigor at the moment.

What do you need now—reflection or rigor?

❧

*G*ALILEO, the scientist who discovered the structure of the universe before the Church was willing to accept the new information, is a lesson for today. Things go so fast sometimes that old answers wear out before new ones can emerge. Do your best; live in the spirit of the gospels, and you will have nothing to fear.

N EWNESS is exciting but not always easy to accept. It often takes a great deal of faith to accept change in life. But then again, newness and change may be one of the few times in life that we really get the chance to believe that God is everywhere, even where we've never been before. Has this been true for you?

※

T HE Desert Fathers and Mothers passed this bit of wisdom to their disciples: "Abba Poemen said about Abba Pior that every single day he made a fresh beginning." We need to make new beginnings, too, if not in our behaviors at least in the way we look at things. If you aren't the kind to make New Year's resolutions, at least try waking up each morning and celebrating your chance to make another new beginning.

※

W E used to have a sister who warned us all to "watch how we word our prayers." Well, today, as part of Church Unity Week, the community prays for faith and knowledge. It's a good day to remember that faith isn't faith until it's all we have to hold on to and knowledge fails us. When we pray for faith, we automatically pray for darkness. Think about it.

❧

*T*HE ancients taught, "Wherever there is excess, something is lacking." We need new respect for self-control in a society smothered by a commitment to license.

*P*ATIENCE and hope are not the same things. Hope is the certainty that in the end, God will work God's will. Patience is what makes hope new, day after disappointing day.

❧

*W*E should strive for more than personal or private values—kindness, hope, gentleness, strength. We are asked, as well, for a new commitment to the peace and unity that bring human development and create a world without hunger, hatred, and violence. Do something today to bring human unity.

*A*MADEUS Mozart brought new beauty and creativity into the world. He was hated for it by jealous contemporaries, but he persisted.

Celebrate people who have the inner strength to go on giving their gifts, no matter who rejects them for it.

❧

*W*HEN Sisters go on a long or difficult journey for serious reasons, they are called to kneel in the center aisle of the chapel to receive a special community blessing. The practice has two effects: it keeps the community aware of the efforts of its members, and it keeps the monastic aware of the support of the community so that no matter how much energy the new work takes, there is never a doubt that we are not alone in it.

❧

*O*NE of the most difficult things in life is to keep on doing a thing when its newness has worn off. Pray for the grace to persevere so that the good you begin can be completed.

*M*AHATMA Gandhi was assassinated by one of his own for attempting to bring peace between religious factions of the new nation of India, which he had helped to unite against British colonialism. It's a lesson in reality. We must never do something in order to be thanked for it, not even by those closest to us.

※

*T*o live the monastic life in a monastery on the edges of windswept Lake Erie makes something very clear: hospitality is not a matter of social gentility or niceness. Here, as it was in biblical desert lands, hospitality is often a factor in physical survival. Too often, if it weren't for the spirit of hospitality in this area, people would freeze to death in stranded cars or in city parks or on broken ice floes or in unheated homes. It is an important lesson for people who live a monastic spirituality. It teaches us that hospitality is a lifeline that is part of the fiber of life.

*E*VERYBODY needs a dream, a desire, a goal in life: to complete a good project, to nourish a relationship, to give the grandchildren a treat. Dreams give us a reason to get up in the morning. Dreams take the cold out of life. Dreams make the whole world a warm and loving place. What is your dream today?

❧

*I*T'S easy to take people into our lives in special circumstances and at special times, on holidays, at parties. But hospitality means that we take in new ideas, even when they comfort us least. What are you avoiding today?

❧

*C*OLDNESS is that quality in life that makes us realize need, and need is a special blessing in otherwise comfortable lives. It reminds us of the people we would rather forget, the permanently needy. Be thankful for one need today.

*I*N 1531 the world got the first sight of Halley's comet, a light shooting across the sky, unpredicted and unpredictable.

Life is like a comet. No one of us can say what the meaning of our life will be. We can, however, decide to give a bright, warm light always, no matter how dark and cold the environment around us.

❧

*T*HE nice thing about cold is that it draws people together. On winter nights we light a fire in the library fireplace or the monastery Great Room and sit there together pretending to be saving money on central heating. Actually, we are simply warming one another with presence and roasted chestnuts. If it weren't cold, it wouldn't happen.

What warmth do the cold things in life, like pain and sorrow and death, bring for you?

❧

*H*SIN Ch'i-ch'i, a twelfth-century Chinese poet, wrote, "To what can we liken human life? Perhaps to a wild swan's footprints on mud or snow before it flies off at random, east or west...." In the deep of winter we find ourselves face to face with the fragility of life, true, but to leave "a wild swan's footprints" behind us is to leave a memory of beauty once present and never to be duplicated again.

What footprint will your life leave? Have you made it yet?

∞

*T*ONIGHT the community will pray First Vespers of the Feast of Saint Scholastica, the twin sister of Saint Benedict and the foundress of communities of Benedictine women. She and Benedict, legend implies, had a strong spiritual relationship. If we can learn anything from the thought of two holy people learning from each other, it is that we all need someone who knows our soul. It is one thing to give spiritual hospitality; it is another thing to be able to receive it.

To whom do you entrust your soul? Your quality of life depends on it.

*P*OPE Gregory the Great wrote of Saint Scholastica, "She could do more because she loved more." Love fuels. Fatigue with no apparent physical base is too often a sign of a loss of love. That's why hospitality is as much a gift received as a gift given.

Take someone into your life. Love will give you new energy in a cold world.

❧

*A*FTER twenty-seven years in prison for his activism against the white apartheid government of South Africa, Nelson Mandela was finally freed in 1990 at the age of seventy. A wasted life, you say? Hardly. Every day that Nelson Mandela sat in a government jail cell, the world outside was fired by his conviction and his courage, until, unable to do a thing, Mandela began an entire movement that could not be stopped. He turned frozen hearts into white heat.

What fires are we lighting for the next generation?

"*W*HAT action shall I perform to attain God?" the seeker asked. "If you wish to attain God," came the response, "there are two things you must know. The first is that all efforts to attain God are of no avail." "And the second?" the seeker asked. "The second is that you must act as if you do not know the first."

The lesson is clear: we cannot expect to act out of love unless we have schooled ourselves in the practices that form it.

❧

*G*ETTING to know ourselves and learning to control ourselves are the two great tasks of life. Don't make up strange and exotic "penances." Simply say *no* to yourself once a day, and you will be on the road to sanctity for the rest of your life.

❧

*T*EMPTATIONS are part of life, part of growing up. We grapple with them often—in some instances for our lifetime—before we come to realize that it is not so much the victory as it is the struggle that is holy.

*T*HE concept of perfection is a trick played upon the spiritually unwary to make them think they can arrive at a point beyond which they need not go.

*T*HE *Encyclopædia Britannica* records the fact that valentines were probably the first greeting cards ever made. Paper valentines date from the sixteenth century. Love is irrepressible, yes, but to succeed, love also needs to be worked at, most of all perhaps when it seems most cold. Hospitality is simply love on the loose.

*S*USAN B. Anthony was a leader in the women's suffrage movement. Thanks to her courage, all the systems of the whole world are learning to be a great deal more hospitable toward women. And yet women still get herded into low-paying domestic work in proportions far beyond either their interests or their abilities. But communities of women religious have been a sign for centuries of the strength and intelligence of women. They began schools, opened hospitals, called attention to all the needs of society, and built and managed their own independent institutions.

History is clear: "Male and female God made them. In God's own image, God made both of them."

◈

A Danish proverb reads, "If there is room in the heart, there is room in the house." Who is there in life that you seem to be able to bear in unlimited quantities? And who is there that you have little room for at all? Try to remember that coldness of heart is always a call to personal growth.

◈

H OSPITALITY is the key to new ideas, new friends, new possibilities. What we take into our lives changes us. Without new people and new ideas, we are imprisoned inside ourselves.

*I*T's only when the temperature falls that we really begin to appreciate heat. All of life is understood only in terms of its opposite. That's why little acts of love are so important in a world full of organized hate. What did you do today to turn hate around?

✌

A life of value is not a series of great things well done; it is a series of small things consciously done.

✌

*W*E all need to see the link between the daily and the divine in our lives, or else we shall separate the very elements that are necessary to our own full development: a commitment to the commonplace and a sensitivity to the cosmic in which we dwell.

*I*F there is anything we don't like, it is finding ourselves alone, either physically or intellectually. Too often, perhaps, we seek support when what we really need is integrity.

When was the last time you found yourself in a very different place than the people around you? And?

ॐ

"*T*ELL me the weight of a snowflake," a coal mouse inquired of a wild dove. "Nothing more than nothing," was the answer. "In that case I must tell you a marvelous story," the coal mouse said. "I sat on a branch of a fir, close to its trunk, when it began to snow, not heavily, not in a giant blizzard, no, just like in a dream, without any violence. Since I didn't have anything better to do, I counted the snowflakes settling on the twigs and needles of my branch. Their number was exactly 3,741,952. When the next snowflake dropped onto the branch—nothing more than nothing, as you say—the branch broke off." Having said that, the coal mouse flew away. The dove, since Noah's time an authority on the matter, thought about the story for a while and finally said to herself, "Perhaps there is only one person's voice lacking for peace to come about in the world."

H OSPITALITY is not kindness. It is openness to the unknown, trust of what frightens us, the expenditure of self on the unfamiliar, the merging of unlikes. Hospitality binds the world together.

✑

K ATHARINE Drexel, the foundress of the Sisters of the Blessed Sacrament for Indians and Colored People, was a Philadelphia heiress who established forty-nine foundations, including Xavier University in New Orleans. This woman didn't let the empty places of life go by; she filled them.

What empty places in life are you filling with the will of God?

✑

W OMEN are the invisible majority of the earth, most of them isolated from help, too many of them living the silence of the oppressed. The function of silence in the life of the privileged is to be able to hear the voices of women and to change things in such a way that being born female is no longer a handicap practiced in the name of God.

*S*OLITUDE and loneliness are not the same thing. Loneliness is the sign that something is lacking. The purpose of solitude is to bring us home to the center of ourselves with such serenity that we could lose everything and, in the end, lose nothing of the fullness of life at all.

When you are alone, are you lonely or are you in solitude? If loneliness is what it's about, what you may need most is the cultivation of the richness of solitude.

❧

*F*REEDOM of spirit is the ability to see all the dimensions of life and to move from one to another without being enslaved by any of them.

❧

*S*ILENCE is an intriguing concept. Only silence enables us to hear. But silence is a very noisy thing. When we finally start to listen to our own garbled selves, as well as to others, we discover how full of static our hearts and minds really are. Silence, the time of coming to inner quiet, is the only chance we have of coming to serenity.

"*W*HAT is love?" Victor Hugo wrote. "I have met in the streets a very poor young man who was in love. His hat was old, his coat worn, the water passed through his shoes and the stars through his soul."

If you lost everything you owned tomorrow, if your whole house were emptied out, would there be anything left that you loved enough to maintain the stars in your soul?

❧

*W*OMEN everywhere know what it is to live in worlds empty of a sense of respect, empty of public achievement, empty of real fulfillment. They are blocked, mocked, ignored, and trivialized. And their daughters face it too. What have you done to ensure that the lives of women are fully human, not gender defined?

❧

*P*EOPLE fear a sense of emptiness. We want to be busy about important things. But emptiness is not necessarily sinister. It is good to empty our lives of the trivial and the superficial so that we can come to the things that last—family, prayer, rich ideas, concern for the global human condition.

"*I*n a dark time," wrote poet Theodore Roethke, "the eye begins to see." The dark times in life are not our enemy. Dark times empty the world of the things that would otherwise distract us from seeing the important things. Enter that darkness with confidence.

❧

*W*isdom is what we learn from experience. What wisdom comes from a feeling of emptiness?

❧

*B*efore we can fill ourselves with something new, we have to empty out whatever it is that is filling our time and our hearts and our minds now. What should you be emptying out of your spirit? What should you be filling it with?

*I*F Western culture resists anything at all, it is silence. We pump sound into every available space: into elevators, on boats, in bedrooms, on city streets. Better to do than to think, I suppose, because if we ever really thought about the world we've created, we might change it. And think of all the people who would lose money on that one.

※

"*I*F you are afraid of loneliness," dramatist Anton Chekhov wrote, "don't marry." Is it possible that the breakdown of so many marriages might really be the result, not of selfishness, but of the propensity to demand from another what we have not been able to develop in ourselves?

※

*O*N the death of his child, Japanese poet Issa wrote, "Dew evaporates and all our world is dew…so dear, so refreshing, so fleeting." Death is about learning to let go in life, yes; but it is also about clinging better to love while we can.

What do you love that you are not loving enough right now?

*E*VERYTHING we do seeds the future. No action is an empty one. That's a scary idea, isn't it?

IN SPRING
Soul Emerges

*T*HERE is always new life trying to emerge in each of us. Too often we ignore the signs of resurrection and cling to parts of life that have died for us.

*I*T'S spring. There is new life beginning everywhere—in the earth around us and, if we will, in our souls. Both kinds of life, however, must be cultivated. Spring is a time to concentrate on developing the lasting values of life, the endless possibilities of life, the clear and certain truths of life, the simple joys of a life lived for higher things.

❧

*W*HAT are we looking at that's wrong in life but never say a word about? And why is that? Has life made us full of fear and empty of values?

❧

*P*ASSOVER is the celebration of God's protection of the Jews during the plagues of Egypt. Every Jew knows that God has used Israel to be a sign of the presence of God in life and that God has saved Israel over and over again in order to enable it to be all that it is meant to be.

We are meant to be God's signs of God too. We are called to be all that we are capable of being. We are all meant to be full of the living presence of God.

Are you full of God? Are you all that you were meant to be?

❧

BENEDICT of Nursia wrote, "Say alleluia always, no matter the time of day, no matter the season of life."

❧

THE use of the Alleluia dates back to the earliest of liturgical formularies, both Jewish and Christian, as an endless chant of joy. In the Christian community it was an expression of praise and a foretaste of eternal gladness. "We are an Easter people," Augustine wrote, "and Alleluia is our cry."

❧

THE monastic knows the truth of Easter. Life is all filled up. We don't need anything else now—and nothing else will suffice.

*S*o much is beyond us: family problems, professional challenges, world events. But we are not excused from the responsibility to respond to them. The effort is up to us; the results are up to God.

❧

*T*HERE are things in every life that need to die. The function of the past is to bring us to the present, not to obstruct it.

What is dying in your life right now? Let it go.

❧

*W*HEN we empty ourselves of our fears—fear of failure, fear of loss, fear of criticism—we become free to do what needs to be done in life.

❧

*A*N ancient saying reminds us: "Music needs the hollowness of the flute; letters, the blankness of the page; light, the void called a window; holiness, the absence of the self." We see emptiness as a loss; but emptiness is the only thing that makes new life possible in us.

*W*HAT isn't in us, we can't give to any one else. But if we are full only of ourselves, we are cutting ourselves off from others. It's simple: if we want to make a connection with other people, we are going to have to empty life of its obsession with ourselves.

❧

*V*INCENT van Gogh, the artist, said once, "The best way to know God is to love many things." That's why we have to fill life with the best: the best of music, the best of art, the best of people, the best of literature, the best of ideas, the best of the spiritual life.

*M*Y community has three hermitages where people can go to empty noise, distraction, and schedules out of their lives so that they can get a better look at what's filling them up. Have you ever given yourself some time-without-time for serious thought about the values and direction of your life?

$\mathcal{T}$HE poet Edna St. Vincent Millay wrote, "My candle burns at both ends; it will not last the night; but ah, my foes, and oh, my friends—it gives a lovely light."

The point of life is not to succeed. The point of life is to die trying.

❧

$\mathcal{T}$HE most stable of relationships change character as they go on. Life is simply one long series of changes, a collection of small deaths. The lesson is to learn from one so that we can live better in the next.

❧

$\mathcal{I}$T is not our job to work miracles, but it is our task to try.

❧

$\mathcal{T}$HE *Titanic*, the double-hulled Cunard ocean liner they said could never sink, went down at sea on its maiden voyage. The world was shocked. We had looked to what could never save us for security. It is a lesson that serves us well from time to time. We live in a nation that routinely puts its faith in technology and science when only the things of the heart and mind, spirit and soul, really give life.

What is saving you at this point in your life?

❧

*W*HATEVER is going on for us now in our lives is where growth and wholeness lie for us. Deal with things; don't just ignore them.

❧

*W*E all have major questions of faith. The goal of life is neither to fear those questions nor to repress them. The goal is to come to see uncertainties as the spots in our life where God enters in. It is trust that counts—not questions, not answers.

❧

*I*F creation has stopped in you, start something new this week: a new hobby, a new relationship, a new book, a new time through the Bible. Life is the ability to start over again.

*I*NDIFFERENCE is the acid of life. It erodes all the spirit that's in us and makes us useless to anyone else. We all have to stand for something, or our souls cease to breathe.

*F*LOWERS are an irrepressible expression of the cycles of life. They bloom and die and bloom again the next year more vibrant than before. Human life is like that too. Every stage dies, and out of it new life springs richer than the stage before it.

Today, if you have a garden, pick a flower for every major stage of your life. If you don't have a garden, go to a florist and buy the flowers. Put them on the table in front of your picture. Celebrate your own deaths and resurrections.

*W*HAT we find in the people we love is what we are looking for in ourselves. To whom do you look for direction in life? What does that tell you about what you need to develop in your own life?

IT is so easy, so natural, to look at the others in our lives as tickets to our own comfort. We expect them to do things for us when, actually, it is what we do for them that is the measure of love. Friendship is our pledge to share the life of the other without expecting reward for ourselves.

What is your definition of friendship?

❧

FRIENDSHIP that controls, smothers, and demands is not friendship at all. It ties us down and eats us up. It saps what it should be supporting.

Do your friendships create you or consume you?

❧

MAY, when flowers burst out of hard patches of wintered land, makes growth look so easy. But do not be fooled; growth is the process of staying with what seems futile and useless and ungiving and barren until it becomes something that we know was worth doing—like raising a child or building a good business or salvaging a marriage or learning to live with only the little things of life to nourish us. Growth is the process of finally finding good where for a while no good seemed to be.

❧

ONE of my favorite remembrances of grade school is the May altar. Every day we said our prayers in front of it; every day we loaded it down with fresh flowers purloined from every yard along the way to school. It was a child's way of growing into the idea that heaven was not without a mother's protection and a woman's care.

This culture has substituted masochism and power for feminine concern and gentleness. Maybe that's why all the violence of our time is such a shock to our systems. It is clearly time for May altars again. We need to be shocked at the savagery we have come to call *defense*.

*A*CCORDING to a magazine article I once read, four out of ten people in the United States turn the television on immediately upon entering a room. I thought of years of monastic silence practiced gently and consciously, and I began to wonder if people can grow to the fullness of what they're meant to be when they are being so constantly bombarded from the outside. With constant noise, is there any possibility of ever hearing what is inside of us waiting to be freed?

❧

*F*OR too long we have put the responsibility for human relationships and values on women who are mothers. Each of us, woman and man alike, married or unmarried, have the responsibility for mothering—soothing, caring for, raising up, giving life to others. The day this idea becomes the coin of the realm, war will cease, abuse and battering will cease, destruction will cease. When we are not mothering, we are not being friend to the world.

*B*RITISH novelist Phyllis Bottome said, "There are two ways of meeting difficulties: you alter the difficulties or you alter yourself meeting them." What we cannot change around us demands a change inside of us.

What are you facing now that you cannot change? What change is it demanding inside of you?

❧

*T*oo many times we insist on loving people the way we want to love them instead of the way they need to be loved. What we cannot give them, we do not want them to get from anyone else and fear that, if they do, they will love us less as a result. What a pitiable definition of friendship.

*S*OMETIMES it happens: you simply meet someone who brings another piece of life to your soul like a missing corner of a jigsaw puzzle. That is not acquaintanceship; that is grace, something designed to provide presence when you consider yourself most alone, some-thing meant to call us to grow in depth, self-understanding, and the healing balm of self-revelation.

❧

*T*HE Arabic proverb teaches, "Get close to the seller of perfumes if you want to be fragrant." The friendships we develop determine the quality of our own souls.

What kind of friends do you choose?

❧

*B*EWARE of false friends, the ones who want you for their own emotional comfort, the ones who never sense the difficulties of your situation, the ones who want to control you, not leave you free. What masquerades as friendship is so often simply emotional dependence with a chain. Remember Goethe's warning, "We are shaped and fashioned by what we love."

*W*HEN souls really touch, it is forever. Then space and time disappear, and all that remains is the consciousness that we are not alone in life.

❧

*S*OMETIMES nothing matters but presence, not time, not conditions, not circumstances. When that is the case, friendship has broken out. Treat it tenderly and consciously and well.

❧

*T*HE Irish call it *Mothering Day*. The title manifests the growth of an idea. The fact is that man and woman alike, parent and guardian alike, friend and stranger alike, must learn to mother. Mothering is the art of releasing what is gentle and loving and patient and receiving in all of us.

Who are all the people who mothered, who nourished, who comforted, you in life? Thank God for them.

*I*T is amazing that the Church's attitude toward Mary has not marked the Church's attitude toward women in general. Perhaps the reason is that we could not see beyond what culture told us that women were and so never really came to conversion. Whatever the reason, we all have a lot of growing to do if the woman, Mary, is ever to be seen as God sees women and saw her.

❧

*I*T is not insignificant that Mary, Queen of Peace, is also Mary of Nazareth and not Mary of Jerusalem or Mary of Caesarea. The most significant woman of all time came from one of the area's most insignificant places. Mary made nothingness visible.

It takes a lot of human growing to find value in the valueless—in small places and simple things and powerless people. But that is the basis for peace, both inside of us and in the world around us.

*R*EAL growth comes when we have learned to make the best out of whatever befalls us in life. It's when we lie down and die under the blows of circumstances that we turn opportunity into poison.

❧

*S*CIENTISTS tell us that there are tiny invertebrates called *water bears* that enter a state of suspended animation to withstand extremely low temperatures or the threat of desiccation or dehydration. Some of these little specimens have been kept for over a year in liquid air at -310°F and then revived.

Nature tells us that we can survive a lot of pressure in life and still grow. Giving up is not the answer to much of anything, is it?

❧

*W*OULD you allow your friend to have another friend, equally loved, equally important to your friend as you are? Or would that threaten your own sense of well-being, in which case, do you need friendship or self-esteem?

$\mathcal{F}$RIENDSHIP is a quality of life that knows no boundaries. Friends who are older than we are bring wisdom and calm to our lives. Friends who are younger bring energy and possibility.

Have you ever had a friend who was far older or younger than you? What did it bring out in you? What did it save in you?

❧

$\mathcal{F}$RIENDSHIPS that are real, friendships that engage the soul, are glimpses into the eternal love of God. When we really love someone else with a love that is total and a love that is true, then we know how God loves us. It is a breathtakingly unbearable discovery, isn't it?

❧

$\mathcal{B}$RITISH novelist and politician Sir Edward Bulwer-Lytton knew what was missing in the world a long time before the women's movement made us look at the emotional deprivations that sexism creates. He taught: "It is a wonderful advantage to a man...to secure an advisor in a sensible woman. In woman there is at once a subtle delicacy of tact, and a plain soundness of judgment, which are rarely combined to an equal degree in man. She will seldom counsel you to do a shabby thing, for a woman always desires to be proud of you." Women friends are good for both women and men.

❧

*L*OVE costs. It does not always feel good. It sometimes depresses. It always challenges. But it never hurts; it never attacks; it never abandons. Love is the only thing that makes family doable after romance has faded and excitement has gone its way.

❧

*T*HE year is over. Whatever we waited for this year either came or it did not. One thing is sure: if what we wanted did not come, something surely came in its place. The temptation is to count the change as loss. Julian of Norwich, the thirteenth-century anchorite, wrote that even sin was "behovable"—necessary, important in life, part of our growth, and an opportunity for union with God. And, not to worry, she says, for "all shall be well and all shall be well and all manner of thing shall be well."

If we are still waiting for something, we must remember that a new year is waiting for us, too, with fresh challenge, virgin promise, rude discovery, and confirming triumphs. Open your hearts to life's new hurdles and simmering victories. Life is waiting for your gift.

$\mathcal{E}$ ACH of us grows through stages in life, sloughing off one after another of them, like a butterfly its cocoon. The purpose is to come out of each more beautiful than when we went into it. That is the purpose, the price, and the power of the cleansing times of solitude, the reflective times of silence.

About the Author

*J*OAN Chittister, international author and lecturer, is founder and director of Benetvision, a research and research center for contemporary spirituality. She is past prioress of the Benedictine Sisters of Erie (PA) and past president of the Leadership Conference of Women Religious. She is a social psychologist with a doctorate in speech-communication theory from Penn State. The recipient of many awards for her work for justice, peace, and equality in the Church, she has written several popular books including *Wisdom Distilled From the Daily; Womanstrength: Modern Church, Modern Women;* and *A Passion for Life: Fragments of the Face of God.* She lives in Erie, Pennsylvania.